How Artists Use

Perspective

REVISED AND UPDATED

PAUL FLUX

Heinemann
LIBRARY

www.heinemann.co.uk/library
Visit our website to find out more information about Heinemann Library books.

To order:
☎ Phone 44 (0) 1865 888066
🖹 Send a fax to 44 (0) 1865 314091
💻 Visit the Heinemann Bookshop at www.heinemann.co.uk/library to browse our
catalogue and order online.

First published in Great Britain by Heinemann Library,
Halley Court, Jordan Hill, Oxford OX2 8EJ, part
of Harcourt Education. Heinemann is a registered
trademark of Harcourt Education Ltd.

Editorial: Clare Lewis
Design: Joanna Hinton-Malivoire
Picture research: Melissa Allison
Illustrations by Jo Brooker/Ann Miller
Production: Julie Carter

Printed and bound in China by South
China Printing Co. Ltd.

13-digit ISBN 978 0 431 16215 7
11 10 09 08 07
10 9 8 7 6 5 4 3 2 1

British Library Cataloguing in Publication Data
Flux, Paul
How Artists Use: Perspective.
701.8'2

Acknowledgements
The publishers would like to thank the following for
permission to reproduce photographs:
AKG, London: Art Institute of Chicago pp. **6**, **7** Bern,
Klee Foundation / © Paul Klee, DACS 2006 p. **21**,
National Gallery, London pp. **18**, **19**, Tate Gallery,
London p. **17**; Art Archive/ © ADAGP. Paris and DACS,
London 2001: p. **16**; Bridgeman Art Library: National
Gallery, London pp. **4**, **14**, Private Collection p. **20**;
Ascending and Descending by M. C. Escher, c.2001
Cordon Art B.V.-Baarn-Holland. All rights reserved:
p. **11**; © Victor Vasarely. ADAGP, Paris and DACS,
London 2006: p. **26**; National Gallery of Scotland,
Edinburgh: p. **12**; National Trust Photographic Library:
Derrick E. Witty p. **13**; 2001 The Museum of Modern
Art, New York: p. **28**, © Allan D'Arcangelo. DACS,
London/VAGA, New York 2006 p. **24**; San Francisco Art
Institute: David Wakely Banco de Mexico, Diego Rivera
and Frida Kahlo Museums Trust p. **9**; SCALA: Collection
Gianni Mattioli, Milan / © Georgio de Chirico.
DACS 2006: p. **15**; Städtisches Museum Abteiberg,
Möchengladbach / © 2006 Andy Warhol Foundation
/ ARS, NY / TM Licensed by Campbell's Soup Co., All
Rights Reserved/ DACS London p. **29**; Yale University
Art Gallery, New Haven, Connecticut/ © El Lissitzky.
DACS 2006 p. **22**.
Cover photograph of *Thunderclouds* by Lou Wall
reproduced with permission of Corbis/Lou Wall.

Every effort has been made to contact copyright holders
of any material reproduced in this book. Any omissions
will be rectified in subsequent printings if notice is given
to the publishers.

Contents

Any words appearing in the text in bold, **like this**, are explained in the Glossary.

What is perspective?

This painting is perfectly flat, yet everywhere it seems to have depth and height. **Perspective** is a way of showing space and distance in a picture. Here we can see far into the distance. Our eyes are drawn towards the window at the back. The artist has even painted an apple and marrow about to fall out of the picture. Can you see them?

Carlo Crivelli, *The Annunciation with Saint Emidius*, 1486

4

Perspective changes the way we see things. Here you can see three simple figures, with lines of perspective disappearing towards the back of the picture. Try measuring the figures. The one at the front looks much smaller, but in fact all three are exactly the same size! No matter how often you look at this picture, the figure at the back will always seem the largest.

Lines of perspective

This is a rainy day in Paris more than 100 years ago. You are walking towards two well-dressed people who do not look at you. Perhaps you will need to move out of their way. Far into the distance people are going about their daily business. The artist has made you a visitor in a great city. But remember, this is only a flat piece of **canvas**!

Gustave Caillebotte, *Paris Street, Rainy Day*, 1877

vanishing point

Gustave Caillebotte used great **skill** in making this painting. The lines of **perspective** give the picture the right depth and make us feel we are actually there. The place where the lines meet is called the **vanishing point**. The picture is very large, over 2 metres (6 feet) high by 3 metres (9 feet) wide, so the people at the front are almost life size! Without perspective this kind of picture would not work.

How the eye sees

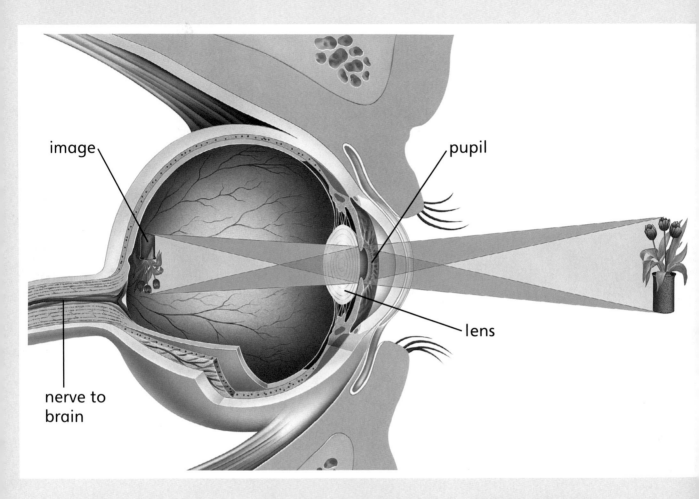

The human eye is very clever. The **image** of what we see passes through the lens and hits more than one hundred million **cells**. These cells send a message to the brain along **nerves**. All of this happens very quickly. Think about how many different images you can see in a minute, and how many messages your brain must be receiving!

Although our brain is very clever it can be fooled by **perspective**.
What is real in this picture? Is the wooden frame part of the
painting? What about the staircase? This picture is in two parts.
If you look at the centre and to the right you see the artist and
his assistants at work, but beyond them is the **mural** which they
are painting.

Tricks of perspective

Perspective is an **illusion**, a trick of the eye. Because of this it is possible to fool the brain into believing something which cannot be true. This figure is called a tri-bar. When you first look at it, it seems quite ordinary. But follow the lines with your finger and you soon realize that the shape is impossible. Your brain wants to see something that is real, and yet it knows that what it is seeing is impossible!

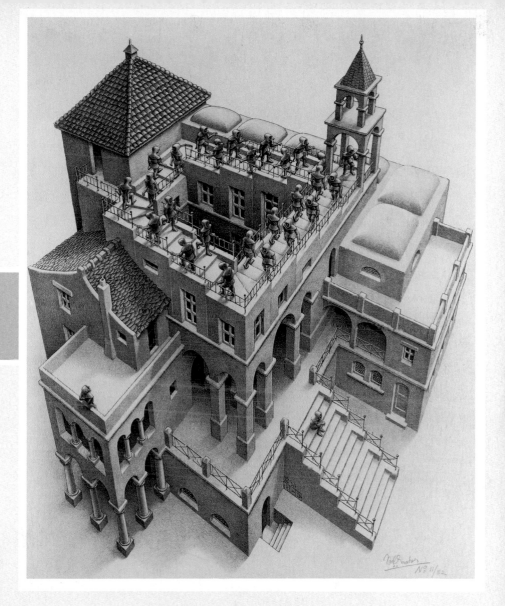

M. C. Escher,
*Ascending and
Descending*, 1960

In this picture you can see many hooded figures going up and
down a staircase. Nothing odd here you may think, but look
carefully. Follow the figures round the staircase with your
eye and you will find that they are going round endlessly.
M. C. Escher has used perspective to trick the brain into seeing
something that cannot be true.

Looking inside buildings

How big do you think this church is? The small people grouped together on the left give you some idea! The artist has used **perspective** to make the church look much bigger than it could possibly be. The building stretches far into the distance. How long might it take you to walk to the end?

Pieter Saenredam, *Interior of St. Bavo's Church*, 1648

Here you can see an open doorway in an old house, looking down a long corridor. But look again. The corridor doesn't really exist. It is just a painting on a flat surface which you can close a door on! Paintings like this are called **trompe-l'oeil**, and were once very popular.

Seeing into the distance

Canaletto painted this picture of Venice on one of the most important days of the year. The ruler of Venice is about to be rowed into the middle of the great **lagoon**. Here he will throw a ring into the water, to bless all the ships that travel in and out of the city. The buildings disappear into the background, giving a sense of great distance. Can you work out where the **vanishing point** is?

Antonio Canaletto, *The Basin of San Marco on Ascension Day*, about 1740

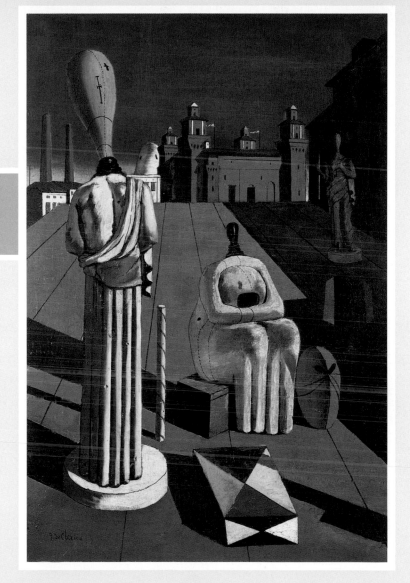

Giorgio de Chirico, *Disquieting Muses*, 1916

What can you see here? A wooden stage with statues and tall buildings in the distance. A strange green light and deep shadows cover a mysterious building. Our eyes look past the central figures to the back of the picture. Have you noticed the box? Objects should get narrower as they go away from us, but this one gets wider.

Perspective, light, and colour

Perspective and colour can be used to create the feeling of open space. This painting shows life inside a railway station. Great billows of smoke swirl around, making it impossible for us to see far. But we know that the railway lines will stretch off into the distance. You can almost hear the engine as it comes towards you!

Claude Monet, *La Gare St. Lazare*, 1877

William Turner, *Rain, Steam, and Speed*, 1844

Here is another early railway **scene**. This time we are out in the open, standing in the centre as a train rushes towards us. The smoke mixes with the cloud and rain to cover the far distance with mist. The space is huge. Even the train seems small here. Can you find the tiny boat? It looks lost in the mist and rain.

Bringing things up close

This is a painting by one of the first artists to study **perspective**. Uccello's paintings did not always work very well because he tried to paint too many things at different **angles**. The people look **wooden** because there is no single **vanishing point**. But parts of it are brilliant! It is very difficult to draw a person lying down from one end, but look at the fallen soldier at the front on the left.

Paolo Uccello, *The Battle of San Romano*, 1450–60

Jan van Eyck, *The Arnolfini Portrait*, 1434

This is a much better use of perspective. The room drifts away from us and the mirror reflects the scene back. We are watching an important moment. It could even be a marriage. The open window reminds us that the real world is just outside. Follow the lines of perspective from the window and you will find the vanishing point. In the mirror are four people: the couple, the artist – might the fourth one be you?

Changing views of perspective

Around 100 years ago some artists began to **experiment** with **perspective**. They painted parts of objects from different **angles** in the same picture. In this painting of a **mandolin** it is as if the artist is saying, "this is what I can see from this position at this moment". This **style** of painting became known as **Cubism**.

Georges Braque, *The Mandolin*, 1909–10

Some artists decided to forget about perspective altogether. Here, Paul Klee has not tried to paint a park as we might see it. He has used **images** of things he has seen in the park and mixed them together. Images of people playing games, trees, flowers, and open spaces make a **decorative panel**, full of life and colour.

How to use perspective

The Russian artist El Lissitzky **experimented** with shapes and patterns. Here a cube seems to float in space, while a sharply **angled** net moves away into the distance. The central column, in contrast, is very flat. The simple shapes and sharp lines of the picture make it look like an **architect's** drawing.

El Lissitzky, *Proun 99*, about 1924

Do it yourself!

1. Mark a **vanishing point** on a piece of paper and draw three or four rectangles.
2. Now join three corners of each rectangle to the vanishing point and colour the shapes in. Do they seem to be coming out of the picture?
3. Experiment with different sizes, shapes, and colours. You could put some flat **abstract** designs in between the shapes, to make your picture more interesting.

How to paint a landscape

Here a modern artist has used **perspective** to create a dramatic **landscape**. The white line of the road disappears away from us. You can almost feel yourself travelling fast along the open highway. The steep lines of perspective give the flat surface a feeling of great depth.

Allan D'Arcangelo, *US Highway 1, Number 5*, 1962

Do it yourself!

1. Cover a large piece of paper with a light blue **colour wash**. Mix in a little white to change the **shades**.
2. Sketch the horizon line low on the paper and put the **vanishing point** in the centre.
3. Draw blocks of different heights, tallest at the sides and getting smaller as you near the vanishing point.
4. Finish off with details of your own. Perhaps you could add an alien spaceship!

Figures in perspective

Compare this picture with the one on page 5. Here the **vanishing point** is in the centre of the white rectangle. The artist has drawn in the lines of **perspective** to make a tunnel. He has drawn three figures coming towards us. Might they be robots from a time in the future?

Victor Vasarely, *Study of Perspective*, 1935

Do it yourself!

1. Draw a square or rectangle near the centre of a piece of paper.
2. Next put in the lines of perspective as shown, with the four lines from the corners slightly thicker.
3. Draw some figures in different sizes. Larger figures should go near the bottom of the page.
4. Shade and colour some of the spaces, making the colours lighter the further back you go. This will make it look like light is coming from the middle of the picture.

27

Making the ordinary different

In this picture Edward Hopper uses **perspective** in a very clever way. Look carefully at the three petrol pumps. In real life they would all be about the same size, but the rules of perspective say that things further away from us should be smaller. The front pump is nearly twice the size of the back one. Look at the size of the house and the man. Do you think the pumps were really as big as they seem here?

Edward Hopper, *Gas*, 1940

Andy Warhol painted these everyday objects in 1962.
The smaller can seems further away because of its size.

Do it yourself!

1. Choose something familiar which you can draw quite
   easily. A jug or cup would be fine.
2. Make three drawings in different sizes, putting the smallest in
   the middle. Does the biggest seem closest to you?

Andy Warhol, *Campbell's Soup Can*, 1962

Glossary

abstract kind of art which does not try to show people or things, but instead uses shape and colour to make the picture

angle the space between two straight lines which meet at a single point, or a viewpoint

architect person who designs buildings

canvas strong woven material on which many artists paint

cell small, simple building block of any living thing

colour wash layer of thin paint which covers a wide area of a picture, usually applied with a large brush

Cubism way of painting, developed by Picasso and Braque, in which objects are shown from different angles in the same picture

decorative panel part of a picture, wall or piece of furniture which has been painted to make it more interesting to look at

experiment to try things out or repeat something until you like the result

illusion something which is not real

image the likeness of a figure or object

lagoon shallow lake

landscape picture of natural and artificial scenery, such as fields, trees, and houses

mandolin kind of musical instrument

mural picture or decoration painted directly onto a wall

nerve very thin cords along which information is passed around the body

perspective way an artist draws or paints on a flat surface, so that there seems to be space and distance in the picture

scene landscape or view painted by an artist

shade a darker or lighter version of a colour

skill ability to do something difficult really well

style the way in which a picture is painted

trompe-l'oeil French for "deceives the eye" – type of painting in which the eyes are tricked into seeing something as real while, in fact, it is painted on a flat surface

vanishing point place in a picture where all the lines of perspective meet and where the picture seems to disappear into the distance. Some pictures may have more than one vanishing point.

wooden figures painted so that they seem too solid, almost like wood

More books to read

Connolly, Sean. *The Life and Work of: Claude Monet*. Oxford: Heinemann Library, 2006.

Connolly, Sean. *The Life and Work of: Paul Klee*. Oxford: Heinemann Library, 2006.

Index